W9-AQM-281

Initiation Rites of the Episcopal Church

THE CHURCH HYMNAL CORPORATION, NEW YORK

Contents

Preface

Holy Baptism is recovering its central place in church life. In a secular and pluralistic age, Christian faith and life are a conscious mature choice. The Catechumenate and the parallel rites for Reaffirmation of the Baptismal covenant have been developed to help people make the conscious mature choice the baptismal covenant represents. This publication helps us see how these rites are related to Baptism. Further, as the use of these other rites grows, we need them together in one book.

Holy Baptism is recovering its central place because it is central to the church's evangelism and all its ministries. To love God and one's neighbor makes us ask what do we believe about our neighbors and what do we believe God wants for them. The baptismal covenant reminds us that to talk of God is to talk of ministry. To evangelize is both to call to faith and to call to ministry.

Mature faith is formed in the congregation, the community of faith. What do we do when a new person comes among us? When we reflect on what we do and what and who the newcomer seeks, we cannot escape Holy Baptism and its rites. How can the newcomer be led into taking on the baptismal covenant? We must provide opportunity for the seeker to make that commitment. That means we must help seekers to learn what it means to live that covenant – to pray oneself, to pray with others, to care for people in need, and to work for justice and peace as one commissioned by God in Jesus Christ to serve and to further God's reign in the world.

Such learning is not a matter of providing books and lectures. We provide a community of support. We provide a community making the same journey following the same leader, Jesus Christ. We provide companions who help these seekers reflect on their experiences. The seekers discover gifts for ministry they had not seen before but which they are already using in their daily places. They learn to cultivate these gifts as part of their spiritual growth. They take on service and justice ministries in the church's name and, even, share their developing faith with nonchurch friends on their own.

There are stages of spiritual growth in this journey toward baptism. Those stages are observed with liturgies that mark the completion of one stage and help the seeker move to the next. When they are baptized and affirm the baptismal covenent, they have already practiced the living of it.

What do we do when a couple is expecting a baby and they tell us they will want to bring the baby for baptism? The baptizing community offers similar experiences for the parents and godparents. Here the focus is on living the baptismal covenant in marriage, family and child-bearing.

The already baptized reaffirming their baptismal covenant travel a parallel path with the community of faith. Some desire a more mature commitment. Some are preparing to reaffirm the covenant in the presence of a bishop for the first time. Some, baptized as infants, want to prepare to make a mature public affirmation of their faith.

As for seekers of baptism, seekers of reaffirmation move through stages in their spiritual journey of preparation. Liturgies likewise mark each stage and help the journey along.

The baptizing community is itself reborn and renewed as it walks the path of dying to the old life and rising to the new life in Jesus Christ with the seekers of life in Christ. The baptizing community completes baptism with the eucharist. Being fed week by week at the table of Jesus Christ becomes a weekly repetition of our baptism for all of us.

For a description of how to implement these rites see *The Catechumenal Process: Formation of Adults for Christian Life and Ministry* by Ann E. P. McElligott and also published by the Church Hymnal Corporation.

The Rev. A. Wayne Schwab
Evangelism Ministries Coordinator

Holy Baptism

Concerning the Service

Holy Baptism is full initiation by water and the Holy Spirit into Christ's Body the Church. The bond which God establishes in Baptism is indissoluble.

Holy Baptism is appropriately administered within the Eucharist as the chief service on a Sunday or other feast.

The bishop, when present, is the celebrant; and is expected to preach the Word and preside at Baptism and the Eucharist. At Baptism, the bishop officiates at the Presentation and Examination of the Candidates; says the Thanksgiving over the Water; [consecrates the Chrism;] reads the prayer, "Heavenly Father, we thank you that by water and the Holy Spirit;" and officiates at what follows.

In the absence of a bishop, a priest is the celebrant and presides at the service. If a priest uses Chrism in signing the newly baptized, it must have been previously consecrated by the bishop.

Each candidate for Holy Baptism is to be sponsored by one or more baptized persons.

Sponsors of adults and older children present their candidates and thereby signify their endorsement of the candidates and their intention to support them by prayer and example in their Christian life. Sponsors of infants, commonly called godparents, present their candidates, make promises in their own names, and also take vows on behalf of their candidates.

It is fitting that parents be included among the godparents of their own children. Parents and godparents are to be instructed in the meaning of Baptism, in their duties to help the new Christians grow in the knowledge and love of God, and in their responsibilities as members of his Church.

Additional Directions are on page 312.

Holy Baptism

A hymn, psalm, or anthem may be sung.

The people standing, the Celebrant says

Blessed be God: Father, Son, and Holy Spirit.
People   And blessed be his kingdom, now and for ever. Amen.

In place of the above, from Easter Day through the Day of Pentecost

Celebrant Alleluia. Christ is risen.
People   The Lord is risen indeed. Alleluia.

In Lent and on other penitential occasions

Celebrant Bless the Lord who forgives all our sins.
People   His mercy endures for ever.

The Celebrant then continues

There is one Body and one Spirit;
People   There is one hope in God's call to us;
Celebrant One Lord, one Faith, one Baptism;
People   One God and Father of all.

Celebrant The Lord be with you.
People   And also with you.
Celebrant Let us pray.

The Collect of the Day

People   Amen.

At the principal service on a Sunday or other feast, the Collect and Lessons are properly those of the Day. On other occasions they are selected from "At Baptism." (See Additional Directions, page 312.)

The Lessons

The people sit. One or two Lessons, as appointed, are read, the Reader first saying

A Reading (Lesson) from _____ .

A citation giving chapter and verse may be added.

After each Reading, the Reader may say

The Word of the Lord.
People   Thanks be to God.

or the Reader may say   Here ends the Reading (Epistle).

Silence may follow.

A Psalm, hymn, or anthem may follow each Reading.

Then, all standing, the Deacon or a Priest reads the Gospel, first saying

The Holy Gospel of our Lord Jesus Christ according to _____ .

People   Glory to you, Lord Christ.

After the Gospel, the Reader says

The Gospel of the Lord.
People   Praise to you, Lord Christ.

The Sermon

Or the Sermon may be preached after the Peace.

Presentation and Examination of the Candidates

The Celebrant says
The Candidate(s) for Holy Baptism will now be presented.

Adults and Older Children

The candidates who are able to answer for themselves are presented individually by their Sponsors, as follows

Sponsor   I present N. to receive the Sacrament of Baptism.

The Celebrant asks each candidate when presented

Do you desire to be baptized?
Candidate I do.

Infants and Younger Children

Then the candidates unable to answer for themselves are presented individually by their Parents and Godparents, as follows

Parents and Godparents

I present N. to receive the Sacrament of Baptism.

When all have been presented the Celebrant asks the parents and godparents

Will you be responsible for seeing that the child you present is brought up in the Christian faith and life?

Parents and Godparents

I will, with God's help.

Celebrant

Will you by your prayers and witness help this child to grow into the full stature of Christ?

Parents and Godparents

I will, with God's help.

Then the Celebrant asks the following questions of the candidates who can speak for themselves, and of the parents and godparents who speak on behalf of the infants and younger children

Question Do you renounce Satan and all the spiritual forces of wickedness that rebel against God?
Answer I renounce them.

Question Do you renounce the evil powers of this world which corrupt and destroy the creatures of God?
Answer I renounce them.

Question Do you renounce all sinful desires that draw you from the love of God?
Answer I renounce them.

Question Do you turn to Jesus Christ and accept him as your Savior?
Answer I do.

Question Do you put your whole trust in his grace and love?
Answer I do.

Question Do you promise to follow and obey him as your Lord?

Answer I do.

When there are others to be presented, the Bishop says

The other Candidate(s) will now be presented.

Presenters I present *these persons* for Confirmation.

or I present *these persons* to be received into this Communion.

or I present *these persons* who *desire* to reaffirm *their* baptismal vows.

The Bishop asks the candidates

Do you reaffirm your renunciation of evil?

Candidate I do.

Bishop

Do you renew your commitment to Jesus Christ?

Candidate

I do, and with God's grace I will follow him as my Savior and Lord.

After all have been presented, the Celebrant addresses the congregation, saying

Will you who witness these vows do all in your power to support *these persons* in *their* life in Christ?

People We will.

The Celebrant then says these or similar words

Let us join with *those* who *are* committing *themselves* to Christ and renew our own baptismal covenant.

The Baptismal Covenant

Celebrant Do you believe in God the Father?
People I believe in God, the Father almighty,
    creator of heaven and earth.

Celebrant Do you believe in Jesus Christ, the Son of God?
People I believe in Jesus Christ, his only Son, our Lord.
    He was conceived by the power of the Holy Spirit
        and born of the Virgin Mary.
    He suffered under Pontius Pilate,
        was crucified, died, and was buried.
    He descended to the dead.
    On the third day he rose again.
    He ascended into heaven,
        and is seated at the right hand of the Father.
    He will come again to judge the living and the dead.

Celebrant Do you believe in God the Holy Spirit?
People I believe in the Holy Spirit,
    the holy catholic Church,
    the communion of saints,
    the forgiveness of sins,
    the resurrection of the body,
    and the life everlasting.

Celebrant Will you continue in the apostles' teaching and
fellowship, in the breaking of bread, and in the
prayers?
People I will, with God's help.

Celebrant Will you persevere in resisting evil, and, whenever
you fall into sin, repent and return to the Lord?
People I will, with God's help.

| Celebrant | Will you proclaim by word and example the Good News of God in Christ? |
| People | I will, with God's help. |

| Celebrant | Will you seek and serve Christ in all persons, loving your neighbor as yourself? |
| People | I will, with God's help. |

| Celebrant | Will you strive for justice and peace among all people, and respect the dignity of every human being? |
| People | I will, with God's help. |

Prayers for the Candidates

The Celebrant then says to the congregation

Let us now pray for *these persons* who *are* to receive the Sacrament of new birth[and for those (this person) who *have* renewed *their* commitment to Christ.]

A Person appointed leads the following petitions

| Leader | Deliver *them*, O Lord, from the way of sin and death. |
| People | Lord, hear our prayer. |

| Leader | Open *their hearts* to your grace and truth. |
| People | Lord, hear our prayer. |

| Leader | Fill *them* with your holy and life-giving Spirit. |
| People | Lord, hear our prayer. |

| Leader | Keep *them* in the faith and communion of your holy Church. |
| People | Lord, hear our prayer. |

| Leader | Teach *them* to love others in the power of the Spirit. |
| People | Lord, hear our prayer. |

Holy Baptism 15

Leader	Send *them* into the world in witness to your love.
People	Lord, hear our prayer.
Leader	Bring *them* to the fullness of your peace and glory.
People	Lord, hear our prayer.

The Celebrant says

Grant, O Lord, that all who are baptized into the death
of Jesus Christ your Son may live in the power of his
resurrection and look for him to come again in glory; who
lives and reigns now and for ever. *Amen.*

Thanksgiving over the Water

The Celebrant blesses the water, first saying

	The Lord be with you.
People	And also with you.
Celebrant	Let us give thanks to the Lord our God.
People	It is right to give him thanks and praise.

Celebrant

We thank you, Almighty God, for the gift of water.
Over it the Holy Spirit moved in the beginning of creation.
Through it you led the children of Israel out of their bondage
in Egypt into the land of promise. In it your Son Jesus
received the baptism of John and was anointed by the Holy
Spirit as the Messiah, the Christ, to lead us, through his death
and resurrection, from the bondage of sin into everlasting life.

We thank you, Father, for the water of Baptism. In it we are
buried with Christ in his death. By it we share in his
resurrection. Through it we are reborn by the Holy Spirit.
Therefore in joyful obedience to your Son, we bring into his

fellowship those who come to him in faith, baptizing them in the Name of the Father, and of the Son, and of the Holy Spirit.

At the following words, the Celebrant touches the water

Now sanctify this water, we pray you, by the power of your Holy Spirit, that those who here are cleansed from sin and born again may continue for ever in the risen life of Jesus Christ our Savior.

To him, to you, and to the Holy Spirit, be all honor and glory, now and for ever. *Amen.*

Consecration of the Chrism

The Bishop may then consecrate oil of Chrism, placing a hand on the vessel of oil, and saying

Eternal Father, whose blessed Son was anointed by the Holy Spirit to be the Savior and servant of all, we pray you to consecrate this oil, that those who are sealed with it may share in the royal priesthood of Jesus Christ; who lives and reigns with you and the Holy Spirit, for ever and ever. *Amen.*

The Baptism

Each candidate is presented by name to the Celebrant, or to an assisting priest or deacon, who then immerses, or pours water upon, the candidate, saying

N., I baptize you in the Name of the Father, and of the Son, and of the Holy Spirit. *Amen.*

When this action has been completed for all candidates, the Bishop or Priest, at a place in full sight of the congregation, prays over them, saying

Let us pray.

Heavenly Father, we thank you that by water and the Holy Spirit you have bestowed upon *these* your *servants* the forgiveness of sin, and have raised *them* to the new life of grace. Sustain *them*, O Lord, in your Holy Spirit. Give *them* an inquiring and discerning heart, the courage to will and to persevere, a spirit to know and to love you, and the gift of joy and wonder in all your works. *Amen.*

Then the Bishop or Priest places a hand on the person's head, marking on the forehead the sign of the cross [using Chrism if desired] and saying to each one

N., you are sealed by the Holy Spirit in Baptism and marked as Christ's own for ever. *Amen.*

Or this action may be done immediately after the administration of the water and before the preceding prayer.

When all have been baptized, the Celebrant says

Let us welcome the newly baptized.

Celebrant and People

We receive you into the household of God. Confess the faith of Christ crucified, proclaim his resurrection, and share with us in his eternal priesthood.

If Confirmation, Reception, or the Reaffirmation of Baptismal Vows is not to follow, the Peace is now exchanged

Celebrant The peace of the Lord be always with you.
People   And also with you.

At Confirmation, Reception, or Reaffirmation

The Bishop says to the congregation

Let us now pray for *these persons* who *have* renewed *their* commitment to Christ.

Silence may be kept.

Then the Bishop says

Almighty God, we thank you that by the death and resurrection of your Son Jesus Christ you have overcome sin and brought us to yourself, and that by the sealing of your Holy Spirit you have bound us to your service. Renew in *these* your *servants* the covenant you made with *them* at *their* Baptism. Send *them* forth in the power of that Spirit to perform the service you set before *them*; through Jesus Christ your Son our Lord, who lives and reigns with you and the Holy Spirit, one God, now and for ever. *Amen.*

For Confirmation

The Bishop lays hands upon each one and says

Strengthen, O Lord, your servant N. with your Holy Spirit; empower *him* for your service; and sustain *him* all the days of *his* life. *Amen.*

or this

Defend, O Lord, your servant N. with your heavenly grace, that *he* may continue yours for ever, and daily increase in your Holy Spirit more and more, until *he* comes to your everlasting kingdom. *Amen.*

For Reception

N., we recognize you as a member of the one holy catholic and apostolic Church, and we receive you into the fellowship of this Communion. God, the Father, Son, and Holy Spirit, bless, preserve, and keep you. *Amen.*

For Reaffirmation

N., may the Holy Spirit, who has begun a good work in you, direct and uphold you in the service of Christ and his kingdom. *Amen.*

Then the Bishop says

Almighty and everliving God, let your fatherly hand ever be over *these* your *servants*; let your Holy Spirit ever be with *them*; and so lead *them* in the knowledge and obedience of your Word, that *they* may serve you in this life, and dwell with you in the life to come; through Jesus Christ our Lord. *Amen.*

The Peace is then exchanged

Bishop   The peace of the Lord be always with you.
People   And also with you.

At the Eucharist

The service then continues with the Prayers of the People or the Offertory of the Eucharist, at which the Bishop, when present, should be the principal Celebrant.

Except on Principal Feasts, the Proper Preface of Baptism may be used.

Alternative Ending

If there is no celebration of the Eucharist, the service continues with the Lord's Prayer

Our Father, who art in heaven,
   hallowed be thy Name,
   thy kingdom come,
   thy will be done,
     on earth as it is in heaven.
Give us this day our daily bread.
And forgive us our trespasses,
   as we forgive those
     who trespass against us.
And lead us not into temptation,
   but deliver us from evil.
For thine is the kingdom,
   and the power, and the glory,
   for ever and ever. Amen.

Our Father in heaven,
   hallowed be your Name,
   your kingdom come,
   your will be done,
     on earth as in heaven.
Give us today our daily bread.
Forgive us our sins
   as we forgive those
     who sin against us.
Save us from the time of trial
   and deliver us from evil.
For the kingdom, the power,
   and the glory are yours,
   now and for ever. Amen.

The Celebrant then says

All praise and thanks to you, most merciful Father, for adopting us as your own children, for incorporating us into your holy Church, and for making us worthy to share in the inheritance of the saints in light; through Jesus Christ your Son our Lord, who lives and reigns with you and the Holy Spirit, one God, for ever and ever. *Amen.*

Alms may be received and presented, and other prayers may be added, concluding with this prayer

Almighty God, the Father of our Lord Jesus Christ, from whom every family in heaven and earth is named, grant you to be strengthened with might by his Holy Spirit, that, Christ dwelling in your hearts by faith, you may be filled with all the fullness of God. *Amen.*

Additional Directions

Holy Baptism is especially appropriate at the Easter Vigil, on the Day of Pentecost, on All Saints' Day or the Sunday after All Saints' Day, and on the Feast of the Baptism of our Lord (the First Sunday after the Epiphany). It is recommended that, as far as possible, Baptisms be reserved for these occasions or when a bishop is present.

If on any one of the above-named days the ministry of a bishop or priest cannot be obtained, the bishop may specially authorize a deacon to preside. In that case, the deacon omits the prayer over the candidates, page 308, and the formula and action which follow.

These omitted portions of the rite may be administered on some subsequent occasion of public baptism at which a bishop or priest presides.

If on the four days listed above there are no candidates for Baptism, the Renewal of Baptismal Vows, page 292, may take the place of the Nicene Creed at the Eucharist.

If desired, the hymn Gloria in excelsis may be sung immediately after the opening versicles and before the salutation "The Lord be with you."

When a bishop is present, or on other occasions for sufficient reason, the Collect (page 203 or 254) and one or more of the Lessons provided for use at Baptism (page 928) may be substituted for the Proper of the Day.

Lay persons may act as readers, and it is appropriate for sponsors to be assigned this function. The petitions (page 305) may also be led by one of the sponsors.

The Nicene Creed is not used at this service.

If the Presentation of the Candidates does not take place at the font, then before or during the petitions (page 305), the ministers, candidates, and sponsors go to the font for the Thanksgiving over the Water.

If the movement to the font is a formal procession, a suitable psalm, such as Psalm 42, or a hymn or anthem, may be sung.

Where practicable, the font is to be filled with clean water immediately before the Thanksgiving over the Water.

At the Thanksgiving over the Water, and at the administration of Baptism, the celebrant, whenever possible, should face the people across the font, and the sponsors should be so grouped that the people may have a clear view of the action.

After the Baptism, a candle (which may be lighted from the Paschal Candle) may be given to each of the newly baptized or to a godparent.

It may be found desirable to return to the front of the church for the prayer, "Heavenly Father, we thank you that by water and the Holy Spirit," and the ceremonies that follow it. A suitable psalm, such as Psalm 23, or a hymn or anthem, may be sung during the procession.

The oblations of bread and wine at the baptismal Eucharist may be presented by the newly baptized or their godparents.

Conditional Baptism

If there is reasonable doubt that a person has been baptized with water, "In the Name of the Father, and of the Son, and of the Holy Spirit" (which are the essential parts of Baptism), the person is baptized in the usual manner, but this form of words is used

If you are not already baptized, N., I baptize you in the Name of the Father, and of the Son, and of the Holy Spirit.

Emergency Baptism

In case of emergency, any baptized person may administer Baptism according to the following form.

Using the given name of the one to be baptized (if known), pour water on him or her, saying

I baptize you in the Name of the Father, and of the Son, and of the Holy Spirit.

The Lord's Prayer is then said.

Other prayers, such as the following, may be added

Heavenly Father, we thank you that by water and the Holy Spirit you have bestowed upon this your servant the forgiveness of sin and have raised *him* to the new life of grace. Strengthen *him,* O Lord, with your presence, enfold *him* in the arms of your mercy, and keep *him* safe for ever.

The person who administers emergency Baptism should inform the priest of the appropriate parish, so that the fact can be properly registered.

If the baptized person recovers, the Baptism should be recognized at a public celebration of the Sacrament with a bishop or priest presiding, and the person baptized under emergency conditions, together with the sponsors or godparents, taking part in everything except the administration of the water.

Catechumenate: Preparation of Adults for Holy Baptism

Concerning the Catechumenate

The catechumenate is a period of training and instruction in Christian understandings about God, human relationships, and the meaning of life, which culminates in the reception of the Sacraments of Christian Initiation.

The systematic instruction and formation of its catechumens is a solemn responsibility of the Christian community. Traditionally, the preparation of catechumens is a responsibility of the bishop, which is shared with the presbyters, deacons, and appointed lay catechists of the diocese.

Principles of Implementation

1. A catechumen is defined as an unbaptized adult. These rites are appropriate for use only with such persons.

2. During the period of the catechumenate, the context of catechesis is a continual reflection on Scripture, Christian prayer, worship, and the catechumen's gifts for ministry and work for justice and peace. These elements are more or less a part of each catechetical session.

3. The principal curriculum for each catechetical session is reflection on the respective readings of the Sunday Eucharistic Lectionary as these illumine the faith journey of catechumens, sponsors, and catechists.

4. The catechetical methodology of the catechumenal and baptismal rites is: experience first, then reflect. As the catechumen journeys from inquiry to baptism, there is formation of an ability to discern God's activity in the events of one's life. It is recommended that the services not be discussed prior to their celebration. It is appropriate that sponsors be well prepared for their ministry in the respective services and to guide and support their catechumen during the celebration.

5. The catechumenate exists throughout the year in the parish, and persons may enter at any time. The catechumenate is of undetermined length for each catechumen. The appropriate time for the call to Candidacy for Baptism is discerned by sponsors, catechists, and clergy on behalf of the local congregation. Baptism of catechumens is normally reserved for the Great Vigil of Easter.

6. Since the catechumenate is ecclesial formation for the ministry of the baptized, it is appropriate that the catechists be representative of the diversity of the local congregation.

7. It is appropriate for those catechumens baptized at the Great Vigil of Easter to join the ministry of sponsor or catechist for new catechumens at the conclusion of the Great Fifty Days.

The Catechumenate is marked by three stages.

Stage 1. The Pre-catechumenal Period. To this stage belong inquirers' classes with sufficient preparation to enable persons to determine that they wish to become Christians. It is a time during which those who have been initially attracted to the Christian community are guided to examine and test their motives, in order that they may freely commit themselves to pursue a disciplined exploration of the implications of Christian living.

Stage 2. The Catechumenate. Entry into the catechumenate is by a public liturgical act (which may take place for individuals or groups at any time) at the principal Sunday liturgy. Normatively, the act includes signing with the cross. To this stage belong regular association with the worshiping community, the practice of life in accordance with the Gospel (including service to the poor and neglected), encouragement and instruction in the life of prayer, and basic instruction in the history of salvation as revealed in the Holy Scriptures of the Old and New Testaments. This stage will vary in length according to the needs of the individual. For those persons who, although unbaptized, already possess an understanding and appreciation of the Christian religion, it might be relatively short.

Each person to be admitted a catechumen is presented by a sponsor who normally accompanies the catechumen through the process of candidacy and serves as sponsor at Holy Baptism.

Admission to the catechumenate is an appropriate time to determine the name by which one desires to be known in the Christian community. This may be one's given name, a new name legally changed, or an additional name of Christian significance.

From the time of admission, a catechumen is regarded as a part of the

Christian community. For example, a person who dies during the catechumenate receives a Christian burial.

Stage 3. Candidacy for Baptism. To this stage belong a series of liturgical acts leading up to baptism. These ordinarily take place on a series of Sundays preceding one of the stated days for baptism, and involve public prayer for the candidates, who are present at the services as a group, accompanied by their sponsors. When the Sacrament of Holy Baptism is administered at Easter, enrollment as a candidate normally takes place at the beginning of Lent; when baptisms are planned for the Feast of the Baptism of Our Lord, the enrollment takes place at the beginning of Advent.

In addition to these public acts, this stage involves the private disciplines of fasting, examination of conscience, and prayer, in order that the candidates will be spiritually and emotionally ready for baptism. It is appropriate that, in accordance with ancient custom, the sponsors support their candidates by joining them in prayer and fasting.

A fourth period immediately follows the administration of Holy Baptism. In the case of persons baptized at the Great Vigil, it extends over the Fifty Days of Easter. This period is devoted to such activities, formal and informal, as will assist the newly baptized to experience the fullness of the corporate life of the Church and to gain a deeper understanding of the meaning of the Sacraments.

The bishop, the bishop's representative, or the rector (or priest-in-charge) of the congregation should preside at the rites of Admission and Enrollment.

It should be noted that the rites and prayers which follow are appropriate for use only with persons preparing for baptism. Validly baptized Christians present at instruction classes to deepen their understanding of the faith, including members of other Christian bodies preparing to be received into the Episcopal Church, are under no circumstances to be considered catechumens. The same is true of persons preparing to re-affirm their baptismal vows after having abandoned the practice of the Christian religion, since "The bond which God establishes in Baptism is indissoluble" (Prayer Book, page 298).

Preparation of Adults for Holy Baptism: The Catechumenate

Admission of Catechumens

The admission of catechumens may take place at any time of the year, within a principal Sunday liturgy.

After the sermon (or after the Creed) the Celebrant invites those to be admitted as catechumens to come forward with their sponsors.

The Celebrant then asks the following question of those to be admitted. If desired, the question may be asked of each person individually.

What do you seek?
Answer   Life in Christ.

The Celebrant then says,

Jesus said, "The first commandment is this: Hear, O Israel: The Lord our God is the only Lord. Love the Lord your God with all your heart, with all your soul, and with all your strength. The second is this: Love your neighbor as yourself. There is no other commandment greater than these." Do you accept these commandments?

Answer   I do.

Celebrant Do you promise to be regular in attending the worship of God and in receiving instruction?
Answer I do.

Celebrant Will you open your ears to hear the Word of God and your heart and mind to receive the Lord Jesus?
Answer I will, with God's help.

The Celebrant then addresses the sponsors

Will you who sponsor *these persons* support *them* by prayer and example and help *them* to grow in the knowledge and love of God?

Sponsors I will.

Those to be admitted kneel. The sponsors remain standing, and place a hand upon the shoulder of the one they are sponsoring, while the Celebrant extends a hand toward them and says

May Almighty God, our heavenly Father, who has put the desire into your *hearts* to seek the grace of our Lord Jesus Christ, grant you the power of the Holy Spirit to persevere in this intention and to grow in faith and understanding.

People Amen.

Each of those to be admitted is presented by name to the Celebrant, who, with the thumb, marks a cross on the forehead of each, saying

N., receive the sign of the Cross on your forehead and in your heart, in the Name of the Father, and of the Son, and of the Holy Spirit.

People Amen.

The Sponsors also mark a cross on the foreheads of their catechumens.

The catechumens and sponsors then return to their places.

The Liturgy continues with (the Creed and) the Prayers of the People, in the course of which prayer is offered for the new catechumens by name.

If any of the catechumens, after consultation with the celebrant, wishes to renounce a former way of worship, an appropriately worded renunciation may be included immediately following the first question and answer.

During the Catechumenate

During this period, and continuing through the period of Candidacy, formal instruction is given to the catechumens. At the conclusion of each session, a period of silence is observed, during which the catechumens pray for themselves and one another. Sponsors and other baptized persons present offer their prayers for the catechumens. The instructor then says one or two of the following or some other suitable prayers, and concludes by laying a hand individually on the head of each catechumen in silence. It is traditional that this act be performed by the instructor, whether bishop, priest, deacon, or lay catechist.

1

O God, the creator and savior of all flesh, look with mercy on your *children* whom you call to yourself in love. Cleanse *their hearts* and guard *them* as *they prepare* to receive your Sacraments that, led by your Holy Spirit, *they* may be united with your Son, and enter into the inheritance of your sons and daughters; through Jesus Christ our Lord. *Amen.*

2

O God of truth, of beauty, and of goodness, we give you
thanks that from the beginning of creation you have revealed
yourself in the things that you have made; and that in every
nation, culture, and language there have been those who,
seeing your works, have worshiped you and sought to do
your will. Accept our prayers for *these* your *servants* whom
you have called to know and love you as you have been
perfectly revealed in your Son Jesus Christ our Redeemer, and
bring *them* with joy to new birth in the waters of Baptism;
through Jesus Christ our Lord. *Amen.*

3

O God of righteousness and truth, you inaugurated your
victory over the forces of deceit and sin by the Advent of
your Son: Give to *these catechumens* a growing
understanding of the truth as it is in Jesus; and grant that
they, being cleansed from sin and born again in the waters of
Baptism, may glorify with us the greatness of your Name;
through Jesus Christ our Lord. *Amen.*

4

O God, in your pity you looked upon a fallen world, and
sent your only Son among us to vanquish the powers of
wickedness. Deliver *these* your *servants* from slavery to sin
and evil. Purify *their* desires and thoughts with the light of
your Holy Spirit. Nourish *them* with your holy Word,
strengthen *them* in faith, and confirm *them* in good works;
through Jesus Christ our Lord. *Amen.*

5

Look down in mercy, Lord, upon *these catechumens* now
being taught in your holy Word. Open *their* ears to hear and

their hearts to obey. Bring to *their minds their* past sins, committed against you and against *their* neighbors, that *they* may truly repent of them. And in your mercy preserve *them* in *their* resolve to seek your kingdom and your righteousness; through Jesus Christ our Lord. *Amen.*

6

Drive out of *these catechumens,* Lord God, every trace of wickedness. Protect *them* from the Evil One. Bring *them* to the saving waters of baptism, and make *them* yours for ever; through Jesus Christ our Lord. *Amen.*

7

Lord Jesus Christ, loving Redeemer of all, you alone have the power to save. At your Name every knee shall bow, whether in heaven, on earth, or under the earth. We pray to you for *these catechumens* who *seek* to serve you, the one true God. Send your light into *their hearts*, protect *them* from the hatred of the Evil One, heal in *them* the wounds of sin, and strengthen *them* against temptation. Give *them* a love of your commandments, and courage to live always by your Gospel, and so prepare *them* to receive your Spirit; you who live and reign for ever and ever. *Amen.*

8

Most merciful God, behold and sustain *these catechumens* who *seek* to know you more fully: Free *them* from the grasp of Satan, and make *them* bold to renounce all sinful desires that entice *them* from loving you; that, coming in faith to the Sacrament of Baptism, *they* may commit *themselves* to you, receive the seal of the Holy Spirit, and share with us in the eternal priesthood of Jesus Christ our Lord. *Amen.*

9

Lord God, unfailing light and source of light, by the death
and resurrection of your Christ you have cast out hatred and
deceit, and poured upon the human family the light of truth
and love: Look upon *these catechumens* whom you have
called to enter your covenant, free *them* from the power of
the Prince of darkness, and number *them* among the
children of promise; through Jesus Christ our Lord. *Amen.*

10

Stir up, O Lord, the *wills* of *these catechumens,* and assist
them by your grace, that *they* may bring forth plenteously
the fruit of good works, and receive from you a rich reward;
through Jesus Christ our Lord. *Amen.*

Enrollment of Candidates for Baptism

*The enrollment of candidates for Baptism at the Great Vigil of Easter
normally takes place on the First Sunday in Lent. For those preparing for
Baptism on the Feast of our Lord's Baptism, it takes place on the First
Sunday of Advent.*

*The large book in which the names of the candidates for Baptism are to
be written is placed where it can easily be seen and used.*

*After the Creed, the catechumens to be enrolled are invited to come
forward with their sponsors.*

*A Catechist, or other lay representative of the congregation, presents
them to the bishop or priest with the following or similar words*

I present to you *these catechumens* who *have* been strengthened by God's grace and supported by the example and prayers of this congregation, and I ask that *they* be enrolled as *candidates* for Holy Baptism.

The Celebrant asks the sponsors

Have they been regular in attending the worship of God and in receiving instruction?

Sponsors   They have. (*He* has.)

Celebrant   Are *they* seeking by prayer, study, and example to pattern *their lives* in accordance with the Gospel?
Sponsors   They are. (*He* is.)

The Celebrant asks the sponsors and congregation

As God is your witness, do you approve the enrolling of *these catechumens* as *candidates* for Holy Baptism?

Answer   We do.

The Celebrant addresses the catechumens

Do you desire to be baptized?

Catechumens   I do.

The Celebrant then says

In the Name of God, and with the consent of this congregation, I accept you as *candidates* for Holy Baptism, and direct that your *names* be written in this book. God grant that *they* may also be written in the Book of Life.

The candidates then publicly write their names in the book; or, if necessary, someone else may write the names. Each name is said aloud at the time of writing. The sponsors may also sign the book.

The candidates remain together at the front of the church while the
Deacon, or other person appointed, leads the following litany:

In peace let us pray to the Lord, saying "Lord, have mercy."

For *these catechumens*, that *they* may remember this day on
which *they were* chosen, and remain for ever grateful for this
heavenly blessing, let us pray to the Lord.
Lord, have mercy.

That *they* may use this Lenten season wisely, joining with us
in acts of self-denial and in performing works of mercy, let
us pray to the Lord.
Lord, have mercy.

For *their* teachers, that they may make known to those
whom they teach the riches of the Word of God, let us pray
to the Lord.
Lord, have mercy.

For *their* sponsor(s), that in *their* private *lives* and public
actions *they* may show to *these candidates* a pattern of life in
accordance with the Gospel, let us pray to the Lord.
Lord, have mercy.

For *their families* and friends, that they may place no
obstacles in the way of *these candidates*, but rather assist
them to follow the promptings of the Spirit, let us pray to
the Lord.
Lord, have mercy.

For this congregation, that [during this Lenten season] it
may abound in love and persevere in prayer, let us pray to
the Lord.
Lord, have mercy.

For our Bishop, and for all the clergy and people, let us pray
to the Lord.
Lord, have mercy.

For our President, for the leaders of the nations, and for all in authority, let us pray to the Lord.
Lord, have mercy.

For the sick and the sorrowful, and for those in any need or trouble, let us pray to the Lord.
Lord, have mercy.

For _____, let us pray to the Lord.
Lord, have mercy.

For all who have died in the hope of the resurrection, and for all the departed, let us pray to the Lord.
Lord, have mercy.

In the communion of [_____ and of all the] saints, let us commend ourselves, and one another, and all our life, to Christ our God.
To you, O Lord our God.

Silence

The Celebrant says the following prayer with hands extended over the candidates

Immortal God, Lord Jesus Christ, the protector of all who come to you, the life of those who believe, and the resurrection of the dead: We call upon you for *these* your *servants* who *desire* the grace of spiritual rebirth in the Sacrament of Holy Baptism. Accept *them*, Lord Christ, as you promised when you said, "Ask, and it will be given you; seek, and you will find; knock, and it will be opened to you." Give now, we pray, to those who ask, let those who seek find, open the gate to those who knock; that *these* your *servants* may receive the everlasting benediction of your heavenly washing, and come to that promised kingdom which you have prepared, and where you live and reign for ever and ever. *Amen.*

The candidates then return to their places and the Liturgy continues with the Confession of Sin or with the Peace.

During Candidacy

On the Sundays preceding their baptism, the candidates attend public worship with their sponsors, and both the candidates and sponsors are prayed for by name in the Prayers of the People. (When Eucharistic Prayer D is used, however, it is appropriate that the names be inserted at the place provided in that prayer.)

In addition, the following prayers and blessings may be used immediately before the Prayers of the People, especially on the Third, Fourth, and Fifth Sundays in Lent (or, the Second, Third, and Fourth Sundays of Advent). When these prayers are used, the candidates and sponsors are called forward. The candidates kneel or bow their heads. The sponsors each place a hand upon the shoulder of their candidate.

The Celebrant then calls the people to prayer in these or similar words

Let us pray in silence, dearly beloved, for *these candidates* who *are* preparing to receive the illumination of the Holy Spirit in the Sacrament of Baptism.

All pray in silence.

The Celebrant says one of the following prayers:

Lord God, in the beginning of creation you called forth light to dispel the darkness that lay upon the face of the deep: Deliver *these* your *servants* from the powers of evil and illumine *them* with the light of your presence, that with open eyes and glad hearts *they* may worship you and serve you, now and for ever; through Jesus Christ our Lord. Amen.

or this

Lord Christ, true Light who enlightens every one: Shine, we pray, in the *hearts* of *these candidates*, that *they* may clearly see the way that leads to life eternal, and may follow it without stumbling; for you yourself are the Way, O Christ, as you are the Truth and the Life; and you live and reign for ever and ever. *Amen.*

or this

Come, O Holy Spirit, come; come as the wind and cleanse; come as the fire and burn; convict, convert, and consecrate the minds and hearts of *these* your *servants*, to *their* great good and to your great glory; who with the Father and the Son are one God, now and for ever. *Amen.*

The Celebrant lays a hand on the head of each candidate in silence.

The Celebrant then adds one of the following blessings:

May Almighty God bestow upon you the blessing of his mercy, and give you an understanding of the wisdom that leads to salvation; through Christ our Lord. *Amen.*

or this

May Almighty God keep your steps from wandering from the way of truth, and cause you to walk in the paths of peace and love; through Christ our Lord. *Amen.*

or this

May Almighty God nourish you with true knowledge of the catholic faith, and grant you to persevere in every good work; through Christ our Lord. *Amen.*

The candidates and sponsors return to their places and the Liturgy continues.

Additional Directions:

1. When there are catechumens who are candidates for baptism at the Great Vigil of Easter, it is appropriate in any year with the consent of the Bishop to use the Sunday lectionary for Year A during Lent and the Great Fifty Days of Easter.

2. In parishes where catechumens are dismissed from the Sunday Eucharist, it is appropriate that this take place following the sermon. The celebrant should send them forth from the Assembly with a blessing and commission to study the Word they have received. Catechumens should be accompanied from the Assembly by their sponsors and catechists to the place for the catechetical session.

3. It is appropriate that the Apostles' (or Nicene) Creed be given to the Candidates for Baptism on the Third Sunday in Lent and the Lord's Prayer be given to them on the Fifth Sunday in Lent following the "Prayers for the Candidates for Baptism" on those Sundays.

Concerning Reaffirmation
of Baptismal Vows

This series of rites and stages of preparation employs a process similar to
that of the catechumenate to prepare mature baptized persons to reaffirm
their baptismal covenant and receive the laying on of hands by the
bishop. It is also appropriate for already confirmed persons who wish to
enter a time of disciplined renewal of the baptismal covenant and for
those who have transferred into a new congregation.

It is important to note, however, that this is not the catechumenate,
which is appropriate only for the unbaptized. In some congregations, it
may be desirable, due to limited resources, for catechumens and the
previously baptized to attend meetings together during each stage.
Care should be taken, however, to underscore the full and complete
Christian membership of the baptized. For this reason, the rites of the
catechumenate are not appropriate for them. During meetings, prayers
offered for the baptized should acknowledge their baptism. Good
examples of such prayers are found in the weekday collects for the Great
Fifty Days of Easter in *Lesser Feasts and Fasts*. When they join the
catechumens in their meetings, the baptized may appropriately be
considered as assisting the catechists.

There are three stages of preparation and formation, each concluding
with a rite as a transition. A final period after the third rite leads to the
Reaffirmation of the Baptismal Covenant at the Easter Vigil and the
presentation of the candidate to the bishop for Confirmation, Reception,
or Commitment to Christian Service during the Great Fifty Days of
Easter. Throughout, the candidate is valued by the community as a living
example of our common need to reexamine and reaffirm our baptismal
covenant, and as a model of conversion.

Lastly, the rites attempt to make full use of the existing symbolic
language of the liturgy, through the use of actions and physical symbols
as well as words.

Stage One. A period of inquiry designed for story sharing and to give persons enough information about Christian faith and practice and the life of the local community so they may determine if they wish to enter a disciplined period of mature formation in the story of God's saving deeds, prayer, worship, and service. At the conclusion of this period, one or more sponsors are chosen from the local congregation.

⎡ RITE ONE   Page 135 ⎤
⎣ **The Welcoming of Baptized Christians into a Community** ⎦

Stage Two. This is a longer period during which those being formed, along with sponsors, catechists, and other members of the community engage in deeper exploration of faith and ministry.

This formation period is based on a pattern of experience followed by reflection. The baptized persons explore the meanings of baptism and the baptismal covenant, while discerning the type of service to which God calls them in the context of the local community. The sponsors and catechists in turn train and support them in that service and help them to reflect theologically on their experience of ministry through the study of Scripture, in prayer, and in worship. Substantial periods of time are spent doing ministry and reflecting on it with catechists and sponsors.

Baptized candidates take part in the Eucharist, including the reception of Holy Communion, unless prevented by penitential discipline.

This rite may also be used to welcome baptized persons who are transferring from another congregation of this Church.

⎡ RITE TWO   Page 137 ⎤
⎣ **The Calling of the Baptized to Continuing Conversion** ⎦

Stage Three. This is a stage of immediate preparation for Reaffirmation of the Baptismal Covenant at the Easter Vigil. The candidates focus on the Lenten disciplines and their role in ministry to others. In their group meetings, candidates for reaffirmation share their on-going experience of conversion — especially with those catechumens who are preparing for baptism — and explore more deeply the life of prayer and ministry.

┌ RITE THREE   Page 138
│ **Maundy Thursday Rite for Baptized Persons in**
└ **Preparation for the Paschal Holy Days** ┐
                                             ┘

The baptized reaffirm their baptismal covenant at the Easter Vigil. It is appropriate for them to join those baptized at the same Vigil in the post-baptismal catechesis during the Great Fifty Days of Easter. If the Bishop was not present at the Vigil, the baptized are presented to the Bishop for the laying on of hands, preferably during the Great Fifty Days as appropriate.

Preparation of Baptized Persons for Reaffirmation of the Baptismal Covenant

The Welcoming of Baptized Christians Into a Community

This rite is used at the principal Sunday Eucharist. It is provided for baptized persons who have been inquiring about life in the community and for those baptized persons who are transferring from another congregation of this Church. Those who wish to pursue a disciplined exploration of the implications of Christian living are recognized by the community and welcomed to begin this process.

During the Prayers of the People, those about to be welcomed are prayed for by name.

After the Prayers of the People, the senior warden or other representative of the community presents the baptized to the celebrant with these or other words:

N., We present to you these persons (or N., N.,) who are baptized members of the Body of Christ and we welcome them to our community as they undertake a process of growth in the meaning of their baptism.

Celebrant (to each baptized person) What do you seek?
Answer Renewal of my life in Christ.

Celebrant In baptism, you died with Christ Jesus to the forces of evil and rose to new life as members of his Body. Will you study the promises made at your baptism, and strive to keep them in the fellowship of this community and the rest of the Church?

Answer I will, with God's help.

Celebrant Will you attend the worship of God regularly with us, to hear God's word and to celebrate the mystery of Christ's dying and rising?

Answer I will, with God's help.

Celebrant Will you join us in our life of service to those who are poor, outcast, or powerless?

Answer I will, with God's help.

Celebrant Will you strive to recognize the gifts that God has given you and discern how they are to be used in the building up of God's reign of peace and justice?

Answer I will, with God's help.

Celebrant *(to the sponsors / companions / friends)* You have been chosen by this community to serve as companions to these persons. Will you support them by prayer and example and help them to grow in the knowledge and love of God?

Sponsors We will, with God's help.

Celebrant *(to the congregation)* Will you who witness this new beginning keep *(N., N.)* in your prayers and help them, share with them your ministry, bear their burdens, and forgive and encourage them?

People We will, with God's help.

The new members remain standing. The sponsors place a hand on their shoulders.

Celebrant *(extending both hands toward the baptized)* Blessed are you, our God, our Maker, for you form us in your image and restore us in Jesus Christ. In baptism, N., N., were buried with Christ and rose to new life in him. Renew them in your Holy Spirit, that they may grow as members of Christ. Strengthen their union with the rest of his Body as they join us in our life of praise and service; through our Savior, Jesus Christ, who lives and reigns with you and the Holy Spirit, now and for ever.

All   Amen.

In full view of all, the baptized write their names in the church's register of baptized persons. The deacon or a sponsor calls out the names as they are written.

Celebrant Please welcome the new members of the community.

People   We recognize you as members of the household of God. Confess the faith of Christ crucified, proclaim his resurrection, and share with us in his eternal priesthood.

The service continues with the Peace. It is appropriate for the new members to greet as many of the faithful as possible. Some may also read the lessons, present the Bread and Wine, and perform other liturgical functions for which they have been previously qualified.

The Calling of the Baptized to Continuing Conversion

This rite is used at the principal service on Ash Wednesday. In it, baptized persons who have been exploring the implications of their baptismal covenant and are preparing to reaffirm it at the coming Easter Vigil are recognized as examples of conversion for the congregation in its journey towards Easter.

After the Blessing of the Ashes and before their imposition, the senior warden or other representative of the congregation presents the baptized to the celebrant with these or other words:

N., We present to you N., N., who have been growing in an understanding of their call as Christians among us and now desire to undertake a more intense preparation to renew their baptismal covenant this coming Easter.

Celebrant Have they studied the promises made at their baptism and strived to keep them in fellowship with this community and the rest of the Church?

Sponsors They have.

Celebrant Have they attended worship regularly to hear God's word and to celebrate the mystery of Christ's dying and rising?

Sponsors They have.

Celebrant Have they joined us in our life of service to those who are poor, outcast, or powerless?

Sponsors They have.

Celebrant Have they strived to recognize the gifts that God has given them and to discern how they are to be used in the building up of God's reign of peace and justice?

Sponsors They have.

Celebrant *(to the baptized)* Will you strive to set an example for us (and especially for those among us who are preparing for baptism) of that turning towards Jesus Christ which marks true conversion?

Answer We will, with God's help.

Celebrant *(to the sponsors)* Will you accompany these candidates in their journey to conversion and help them to renew their commitment to Christ?

Sponsors We will, with God's help.

In full view of the congregation, the candidates kneel or bow their heads. Their sponsors stand behind them and place a hand on their shoulders.

Celebrant *(extending both hands towards the candidates)* Blessed are you, our God, our Maker, for you faithfully call us to return to you and do not abandon us to our own selfishness. You have given N., N., to us as examples of our reliance on you. Renew your Holy Spirit in them that they may lead us in our turning back to you as they prepare to celebrate with us Christ's passage from death to life, who lives and reigns with you and the Holy Spirit, one God, now and for ever.

Answer Amen.

The candidates stand.

Celebrant Receive ashes as a symbol of repentance and conversion and show us by your example how to turn to Christ.

The Celebrant imposes ashes on the candidates using the words of imposition on page 265 of the Book of Common Prayer.

The candidates join the celebrant in imposing ashes on the congregation.

The second Preface of Lent is used.

During the Lenten season, the candidates are prayed for by name at the Prayers of the People, separately from any catechumens.

Maundy Thursday Rite of Preparation for the Paschal Holy Days

This rite is used at the principal service on Maundy Thursday. In it, baptized persons who have been preparing for reaffirmation of their baptismal covenant at the Easter Vigil are further recognized as members so they may join the community in its Paschal celebration.

When this rite is used, the appropriate Gospel is John 13:1-15. Before the foot-washing ceremony, the candidates for reaffirmation and their sponsors stand before the celebrant in full view of the congregation.

Celebrant   *(to the candidates and their sponsors)* N., N., you have been setting an example for us of that true turning to God which lies at the heart of our Christian calling. Tonight we welcome you to join us as disciples of Jesus Christ by imitating his example and dedicating ourselves to service among us in this community. Christ Jesus came among us not to be served but to serve. Tonight we wash your feet as a sign of the servanthood to which Christ has called us and we ask you in turn to join us in this symbol of our discipleship. N., N., are you prepared to join us in our life of service?

Candidates We are prepared.

The service continues with a rite of reconciliation, beginning on page 450 of the Book of Common Prayer *with the words, "Now in the presence of Christ . . . ," omitting the confession of particular sins ("Especially . . ."). The celebrant lays a hand on each candidate while saying the first form of absolution ("Our Lord . . . who offered . . .").*

The candidates' feet are washed. When all are ready, the celebrant distributes basins, ewers, and towels to the candidates, saying to each:

Celebrant May Christ strengthen you in the service which he
lays upon you.

*The candidates in turn wash the feet of other members of the
congregation.*

*The service proceeds immediately with the Peace. It is appropriate to use
Eucharistic Prayer D, including in it intercessions for the Church and for
the world.*

The Preparation of Parents and Godparents for the Baptism of Infants and Young Children

Concerning the Service

This process is designed to deepen the Christian formation of those who will present infants and young children for baptism. Its division into stages — each concluding with a rite — parallels the form of the catechumenate. It is essential, however, that these persons be distinguished from the catechumens except when they may be themselves preparing for baptism, and therefore catechumens.

Stage One. This stage begins as soon as the parents discover the pregnancy. In consultation with the pastor, they choose godparents. The godparents must be baptized persons and at least one a member of the local community. A schedule of meetings throughout the pregnancy is planned. This is a brief stage, leading shortly to the first rite.

[
RITE ONE
The Blessing of Parents at the Beginning of the Pregnancy
]

This rite "The Blessing of a Pregnant Woman," appears on page 153. In order to more strongly indicate the role of the father, the following changes should be made, in addition to changing the title. (If the father is not present or not involved, the rite follows the form for a woman, omitting the father's name in the prayers.)

In the opening prayer, the father's name as well as the mother's is used, and "they" replaces "she."

After the fourth petition is added:

Blessed are you, our God. May N. and N., along with their child's godparents, N. and N. (and N. and N., their other children), find their faith deepened and their ministry strengthened as they prepare for this child's birth and baptism. Amen.

This rite takes place at the Sunday Eucharist after the Prayers of the People. It is followed by the Peace.

Stage Two. This period consists of the remainder of the pregnancy and the time of birth. During this stage, the parents, their other children, and the godparents meet regularly with one or more catechists to deepen their formation in salvation history, prayer, worship, and social ministry. Its educational pattern is one of experience followed by reflection. In their daily lives, participants find ample resources for reflection upon the ways in which their own baptismal covenant is being lived within their vocation of marriage, family and child-bearing. They also explore prayer and worship in the home as an extension of the liturgy of the Church and in the context of the Church Year, and they grow in an understanding of the household as a domestic manifestation of the People of God whose life together is part of the history of salvation.

If a parent is a catechumen, this process takes place within the catechumenate. A baptized spouse may serve to sponsor the catechumen.

RITE TWO
Thanksgiving for the Birth or Adoption of a Child

This rite is found in the Book of Common Prayer (pages 439-445). Of the final prayers, the prayer "For a child not yet baptized" (page 444) is appropriate. The celebrant signs the infant with the cross and announces the date of the baptism. Henceforth the child is prayed for by name at the Prayers of the People, until the baptismal day.

Stage Three. In this period of preparation for baptism, the parents and godparents continue to meet with the catechist(s). Couples or individuals who have raised children in the Church may be helpful as resources or catechists, as may be others who have completed this process previously. The experience of parenthood furnishes new challenges to faith and ministry upon which reflection will be fruitful. The process of family life, sharing in the congregation's life of worship, and ministry to others will find new shape with the advent of the new child.

This is also a time to explore more fully the responsibilities that the parents and godparents will accept at the baptism. They explore topics such as: the best way to interpret the meaning of the Eucharist to a child partaking of it in his or her growing years; how to model ministry and prayer for the growing child; and ways of introducing the child to the story of salvation. The role of the godparents is also more fully developed.

⌈ RITE THREE   Book of Common Prayer, Page 299 ⌉
⌊ **Holy Baptism** ⌋

In accordance with the Book of Common Prayer, this will take place on a major baptismal day at a principal service of worship. The infant will be signed (with chrism, if desired) and may receive Holy Communion (in the form of a few drops of wine if the child is not yet weaned).

After this, the parents, godparents and congregation have the responsibility of carrying out the child's formation in salvation history, prayer, worship, and social ministry. Childhood and adolescence will be a time of formation and exploration of the mysteries of the faith, moving towards the goal of reaffirmation of the baptismal covenant at a mature age.

Those who lead this preparation process should include laity and clergy. Deacons have a special role as leaders of servant ministry, as do those who have reared children in the Church, even if they seem to have had little success. Whenever possible, the bishop should preside over the rites and take part in the teaching. The bishop will also preside at the baptism whenever possible.

Adaptation for Special Circumstances

Deferred Baptism

In the case of young children, the parents may, in consultation with the pastor of the congregation, determine to defer baptism until the child is old enough to go through the catechumenate. In such case, parents go through the same process during the pregnancy and birth, but the stages conclude not with baptism but with the admission of the child to the catechumenate (page 115). The parents and godparents should receive ongoing support in the formation of the child.

Other Adaptations

When parents present a child for baptism without having gone through this process beginning at pregnancy, the first and second stages above are combined. The first rite is dropped and the second rite is the enrollment of the child as a candidate for baptism (adapted to circumstances). After a final period of preparation (perhaps along with adult candidates), the child is baptized.

It is important to acknowledge that, if a difficulty arises during the course of the pregnancy, the godparents and catechists are the primary ministers to the parents. If the pregnancy is terminated by miscarriage, or if the baby is stillborn, these persons continue to support and assist the parents in dealing with such an event.

It should be noted that a baby with congenital deficiencies (including mental or learning disabilities) should be baptized. In cases where it seems necessary to perform an emergency baptism, the sponsoring group supports the parents. If the infant survives, the formative period may continue and the formal celebration of the baptism takes place on a major baptismal day.

Confirmation

Concerning the Service

In the course of their Christian development, those baptized at an early age are expected, when they are ready and have been duly prepared, to make a mature public affirmation of their faith and commitment to the responsibilities of their Baptism and to receive the laying on of hands by the bishop.

Those baptized as adults, unless baptized with laying on of hands by a bishop, are also expected to make a public affirmation of their faith and commitment to the responsibilities of their Baptism in the presence of a bishop and to receive the laying on of hands.

When there is no Baptism, the rites of Confirmation, Reception, and the Reaffirmation of Baptismal Vows are administered in the following form.

If desired, the hymn Gloria in excelsis may be sung immediately after the opening versicles and before the salutation "The Lord be with you."

The Nicene Creed is not used at this service.

It is appropriate that the oblations of bread and wine be presented by persons newly confirmed.

Confirmation
with forms for Reception and for the Reaffirmation of Baptismal Vows

A hymn, psalm, or anthem may be sung.

The people standing, the Bishop says

      Blessed be God: Father, Son, and Holy Spirit.
People   And blessed be his kingdom, now and for ever. Amen.

In place of the above, from Easter Day through the Day of Pentecost

      Alleluia. Christ is risen.
People   The Lord is risen indeed. Alleluia.

In Lent and on other penitential occasions

Bishop   Bless the Lord who forgives all our sins.
People   His mercy endures for ever.

The Bishop then continues

      There is one Body and one Spirit;
People   There is one hope in God's call to us;
Bishop   One Lord, one Faith, one Baptism;
People   One God and Father of all.

Bishop   The Lord be with you.
People   And also with you.
Bishop   Let us pray.

The Collect of the Day

People   **Amen.**

At the principal service on a Sunday or other feast, the Collect and Lessons are properly those of the Day. At the discretion of the bishop, however, the Collect (page 203 or 254) and one or more of the Lessons provided "At Confirmation" (page 929) may be substituted.

The Lessons

The people sit. One or two Lessons, as appointed, are read, the Reader first saying

A Reading (Lesson) from _____.

A citation giving chapter and verse may be added.

After each Reading the Reader may say

The Word of the Lord.
People   Thanks be to God.

or the Reader may say   Here ends the Reading (Epistle).

Silence may follow.

A Psalm, hymn, or anthem may follow each Reading.

Then, all standing, the Deacon or a Priest reads the Gospel, first saying

The Holy Gospel of our Lord Jesus Christ according to _____.
People   Glory to you, Lord Christ.

        The Gospel of the Lord.

People   Praise to you, Lord Christ.

The Sermon

Presentation and Examination of the Candidates

The Bishop says

The Candidate(s) will now be presented.

Presenters I present *these persons* for Confirmation.

or   I present *these persons* to be received into this Communion.

or   I present *these persons* who *desire* to reaffirm *their* baptismal vows.

The Bishop asks the candidates

Do you reaffirm your renunciation of evil?

Candidate I do.

Bishop

Do you renew your commitment to Jesus Christ?

Candidate

I do, and with God's grace I will follow him as my Savior and Lord.

After all have been presented, the Bishop addresses the congregation, saying

Will you who witness these vows do all in your power to support *these persons* in *their* life in Christ?

People   We will.

The Bishop then says these or similar words

Let us join with *those* who *are* committing *themselves* to Christ and renew our own baptismal covenant.

The Baptismal Covenant

Bishop   Do you believe in God the Father?
People   I believe in God, the Father almighty,
        creator of heaven and earth.

Bishop   Do you believe in Jesus Christ, the Son of God?
People   I believe in Jesus Christ, his only Son, our Lord.
        He was conceived by the power of the Holy Spirit
           and born of the Virgin Mary.
        He suffered under Pontius Pilate,
           was crucified, died, and was buried.
        He descended to the dead.
        On the third day he rose again.
        He ascended into heaven,
           and is seated at the right hand of the Father.
        He will come again to judge the living and the dead.

Bishop   Do you believe in God the Holy Spirit?
People   I believe in the Holy Spirit,
        the holy catholic Church,
        the communion of saints,

the forgiveness of sins,
the resurrection of the body,
and the life everlasting.

Bishop   Will you continue in the apostles' teaching and fellowship, in the breaking of bread, and in the prayers?

People   I will, with God's help.

Bishop   Will you persevere in resisting evil, and, whenever you fall into sin, repent and return to the Lord?

People   I will, with God's help.

Bishop   Will you proclaim by word and example the Good News of God in Christ?

People   I will, with God's help.

Bishop   Will you seek and serve Christ in all persons, loving your neighbor as yourself?

People   I will, with God's help.

Bishop   Will you strive for justice and peace among all people, and respect the dignity of every human being?

People   I will, with God's help.

Prayers for the Candidates

The Bishop then says to the congregation

Let us now pray for *these persons* who *have* renewed *their* commitment to Christ.

The petitions on pages 305-306 may be used.

A period of silence follows.

Then the Bishop says

Almighty God, we thank you that by the death and resurrection of your Son Jesus Christ you have overcome sin and brought us to yourself, and that by the sealing of your Holy Spirit you have bound us to your service. Renew in *these* your *servants* the covenant you made with *them* at *their* Baptism. Send *them* forth in the power of that Spirit to perform the service you set before *them*; through Jesus Christ your Son our Lord, who lives and reigns with you and the Holy Spirit, one God, now and for ever. *Amen.*

For Confirmation

The Bishop lays hands upon each one and says

Strengthen, O Lord, your servant N. with your Holy Spirit; empower *him* for your service; and sustain *him* all the days of *his* life. *Amen.*

or this

Defend, O Lord, your servant N. with your heavenly grace, that *he* may continue yours for ever, and daily increase in your Holy Spirit more and more, until *he* comes to your everlasting kingdom. *Amen.*

For Reception

N., we recognize you as a member of the one holy catholic and apostolic Church, and we receive you into the fellowship of this Communion. God, the Father, Son, and Holy Spirit, bless, preserve, and keep you. *Amen.*

For Reaffirmation

N., may the Holy Spirit, who has begun a good work in you, direct and uphold you in the service of Christ and his kingdom. *Amen.*

The Bishop concludes with this prayer

Almighty and everliving God, let your fatherly hand ever be over *these* your *servants*; let your Holy Spirit ever be with *them*; and so lead *them* in the knowledge and obedience of your Word, that *they* may serve you in this life, and dwell with you in the life to come; through Jesus Christ our Lord. *Amen.*

The Peace is then exchanged

Bishop   The peace of the Lord be always with you.
People   And also with you.

The service then continues with the Prayers of the People or the Offertory of the Eucharist, at which the Bishop should be the principal celebrant.

If there is no celebration of the Eucharist, the service continues with the Lord's Prayer and such other devotions as the Bishop may direct.

The Bishop may consecrate oil of Chrism for use at Baptism, using the prayer on page 307.